QUICK & EASY

STIR-FRY

RECIPES

Ready in 30 Minutes or Less

PUBLICATIONS INTERNATIONAL, LTD.

Recipe Development: Lucy Wing

Photography: Photo/Kevin Smith, Chicago

Pictured on the front cover: Stir-Fried Chicken with Broccoli (*page 57*).

Pictured on the back cover (*clockwise from top left*): Stir-Fried Broccoli (*page 80*), Normandy Pork and Cabbage (*page 37*), Mandarin Tomato Beef (*page 20*) and Gingered Fish with Bok Choy (*page 67*).

The 30 minutes or less time includes the amount of time it takes to prepare and cook the recipe. The time is for such tasks as opening cans, peeling and chopping vegetables and shredding cheese, as well as stir-frying, simmering and browning. Whenever possible, steps are combined to save time (i.e., vegetables chopped while waiting for water to boil, etc.). However, the 30 minutes or less time does not include the time it takes for advanced preparation of foods (i.e., steaming vegetables, cooking and cooling rice or pasta, thawing vegetables, etc.). All recipes were kitchen tested to insure that they can be prepared in 30 minutes or less.

ISBN: 0-7853-0945-4

Manufactured in U.S.A.

8 7 6 5 4 3 2 1

QUICK & EASY
STIR-FRY
RECIPES

Ready in 30 Minutes or Less

STIR-FRY BASICS

When we think of stir-fries, we generally think of only Chinese cooking—until now! *Quick & Easy Stir-Fry Recipes* brings you an outstanding collection of recipes from traditional Oriental favorites to those with a different twist. Whether it's Asian Ginger Glazed Pork or Monterey Potato Hash, these dishes are sure to delight. Preparing tasty and attractive stir-fry dishes is a rewarding experience that is easy to accomplish. Before you begin, take a few minutes to read through this information to assure sensational results every time.

Stir-frying is a rapid-cooking method invented by the Chinese. It is the brisk cooking of small pieces of ingredients in hot oil over intense heat for a short time, usually just for a few minutes. During cooking, the ingredients must be kept in constant motion by stirring or vigorous tossing. Once cooking is completed, the food should be removed immediately from the heat. In addition to saving time, the quick cooking preserves the nutrients, flavors, textures and colors of the food.

When stir-frying, all ingredients must be well organized and prepared *before the cooking is started*. They should be measured or weighed, cleaned, chopped, sliced and combined. Like ingredients should be cut into pieces of approximately the same size for even cooking. Otherwise, ingredients such as vegetables may be overcooked while meats remain undercooked. The stir-frying is accomplished so quickly that there is usually not enough time to complete any preparation steps once cooking has begun.

Stir-frying should be divided into two steps—preparing the ingredients and cooking the ingredients.

One very useful utensil for stir-frying is a wok. Traditionally, a wok was made from thin, tempered iron and had a rounded bottom for fast, even conduction of heat. However, in addition to iron, woks are now manufactured with aluminum, stainless steel and carbon steel. Woks with flat bottoms are made for use on electric ranges and on smooth-top cooking surfaces. There are also electric woks with nonstick finishes and automatic thermostatic controls. On some woks, the customary thin metal handles positioned on two sides have been replaced with a single long handle. This handle eliminates the necessity of keeping pot holders handy to pick up or steady the wok.

Woks range from 12 to 24 inches in diameter. The 14-inch wok is a good choice because it can handle most cooking techniques without interfering with other burners.

Before a new iron or carbon steel wok is used, it should be washed and seasoned. Wash it in hot, soapy water (the first time only).

Rinse the wok with water and dry it completely. Rub 1 tablespoon of vegetable oil completely over the interior of the wok. Place it over low heat until hot throughout, 3 to 5 minutes; remove from the heat and let it cool. After each use, the wok should be soaked in hot water and cleaned with a bamboo brush or a sponge. *Do not clean the wok with soap or soap-treated scouring pads.* Rinse the wok with water, dry it and place over low heat until all the water evaporates. Rub 1 teaspoon vegetable oil over the inside to prevent rusting. Follow manufacturer's instructions for care of other types of woks, such as nonstick or electric woks. If you do not have a wok, a large, deep skillet can be used.

The kind of oil used is also crucial for successful stir-frying. A vegetable oil that may be heated to a high temperature without smoking is essential. Peanut, corn, canola and soybean oils all work well.

Due to variables such as types of foods, heat and cooking equipment used, cooking times given in this publication should be used as guidelines—not as absolutes.

BUSY-DAY BEEF

THREE–PEPPER STEAK

1 pound boneless beef top round or
   flank steak
3 tablespoons low sodium soy sauce
1 tablespoon cornstarch
1 tablespoon brown sugar
1½ teaspoons sesame oil
¼ teaspoon crushed red pepper

1 small green bell pepper
1 small red bell pepper
1 small yellow bell pepper
1 medium onion
2 cloves garlic
3 tablespoons vegetable oil, divided
   Hot cooked rice

• Cut beef across prominent grain into ¼-inch-thick slices. Combine soy sauce, cornstarch, sugar, sesame oil and crushed red pepper in large bowl; stir until smooth. Add beef and toss to coat. Set aside.

• Cut green, red and yellow peppers lengthwise in half. Remove stems and seeds. Rinse, dry and cut into ½-inch strips. Cut onion in half, then into 1-inch pieces. Finely chop garlic. Set aside.

• Heat wok over high heat about 1 minute or until hot. Drizzle 1 tablespoon vegetable oil into wok and heat 30 seconds. Add pepper strips and stir-fry until crisp-tender. Remove to large bowl. Add 1 tablespoon vegetable oil and half of beef mixture to wok. Stir-fry until well browned. Remove beef to bowl with peppers. Repeat with remaining 1 tablespoon vegetable oil and beef mixture. Reduce heat to medium.

• Add onion and stir-fry about 3 minutes or until softened. Add garlic and stir-fry 30 seconds. Return beef, peppers and any accumulated juices to wok; heat through. Spoon rice into serving dish; top with beef and vegetable mixture.

Makes 4 servings

Three-Pepper Steak

CANTONESE TOMATO BEEF

1 pound fresh Chinese-style thin
    wheat noodles *or* 12 ounces
    dry spaghetti
2 pounds ripe tomatoes, cored
3 small onions
1 small beef flank steak or filet
    mignon tail (about 1 pound)
2 tablespoons sesame oil, divided
2 tablespoons soy sauce

1 tablespoon plus 1 teaspoon
    cornstarch, divided
1 cup beef broth
2 tablespoons brown sugar
1 tablespoon cider vinegar
2 tablespoons vegetable oil, divided
1 tablespoon minced fresh ginger
1 green onion with tops, diagonally
    cut into thin slices

• Cook noodles in stockpot according to package directions just until tender. Meanwhile, cut each tomato into 8 wedges. Cut each onion into 8 wedges. Set aside.

• Cut beef lengthwise in half. Cut across prominent grain into 2 × 1/4-inch slices.

• Drain noodles in colander and return to stockpot. Add 1 tablespoon sesame oil; toss until well coated. Set aside and cover to keep warm.

• Combine soy sauce, remaining 1 tablespoon sesame oil and 1 teaspoon cornstarch in large bowl; stir until smooth. Add beef and toss to coat. Set aside.

• Combine broth, sugar, remaining 1 tablespoon cornstarch and vinegar in small bowl; stir until smooth. Set aside.

• Heat wok over high heat about 1 minute or until hot. Drizzle 1 tablespoon vegetable oil into wok and heat 30 seconds. Add ginger and stir-fry about 30 seconds or until fragrant. Add beef mixture and stir-fry 5 minutes or until lightly browned. Remove beef mixture to large bowl and set aside. Reduce heat to medium.

• Add remaining 1 tablespoon vegetable oil to wok. Add onion wedges; cook and stir about 2 minutes or until tender. Stir in half of tomatoes. Stir broth mixture until smooth and add to wok. Cook and stir until sauce boils and thickens.

• Return beef and any accumulated juices to wok. Add remaining tomatoes; cook and stir until heated through. Transfer noodles to shallow serving bowl. Spoon beef mixture over noodles. Sprinkle with green onion. *Makes 4 servings*

*F*resh *Chinese-style thin wheat noodles can be found in the Oriental food section of large supermarkets or at an Oriental specialty food store.*

Cantonese Tomato Beef

BEEF BENIHANA

1 pound boneless beef sirloin or
  tenderloin, cut 1 inch thick
2 medium zucchini
1 large onion
1 tablespoon sesame seeds
2 tablespoons vegetable oil, divided

½ pound sliced mushrooms
3 tablespoons teriyaki sauce
1 teaspoon sugar
½ teaspoon salt
¼ teaspoon ground black pepper
  Hot cooked rice

•Trim fat from beef; discard. Slice beef across prominent grain into ¼-inch-thick slices. Rinse zucchini; cut off ends. Cut each zucchini crosswise and lengthwise in half. Cut pieces lengthwise into ½-inch strips. Cut onion lengthwise in half and slice crosswise into ¼-inch slices.

•Heat wok over high heat about 1 minute or until hot. Add sesame seeds and cook until lightly browned. Remove to small bowl. Drizzle 1 tablespoon oil into wok and heat 30 seconds. Add beef and stir-fry about 2 minutes or until well browned on outside and rare on inside. Remove beef to large bowl. Reduce heat to medium.

•Add remaining 1 tablespoon oil to wok. Add mushrooms, zucchini and onion; stir-fry about 5 minutes or until vegetables are crisp-tender. Stir in teriyaki, sugar, salt and pepper. Return beef and any accumulated juices to wok; heat through. Spoon rice onto serving plate; top with beef mixture. Sprinkle with sesame seeds.

Makes 4 servings

BEEF À LA STROGANOFF

1¼ pounds boneless beef sirloin *or*
    2 boneless shell steaks
  1 large onion
  1 tablespoon butter or margarine
  2 tablespoons water
  ½ pound sliced mushrooms
  2 tablespoons all-purpose flour
  1 cup beef broth

¼ cup dry red wine
¼ teaspoon salt
1 cup low fat or nonfat sour cream
¼ teaspoon dried dill weed
  Hot cooked noodles (optional)
  Fresh dill sprigs *or* chopped fresh
    parsley for garnish

•Trim fat from beef; discard. Slice beef across prominent grain into thin slices. Cut onion lengthwise in half and slice crosswise into ¼ inch slices.

•Heat wok over medium-high heat until hot. Add butter and swirl to coat bottom. Add beef and stir-fry about 2 minutes or until well browned. Remove beef to large bowl. Reduce heat to medium.

•Add water, mushrooms and onion. Stir-fry about 2 minutes or until onion is tender. Add flour and mix well. Gradually stir in broth, wine and salt. Heat to a boil. Reduce heat to low; simmer 5 minutes.

•Stir sour cream and dill weed into mushroom mixture. Return beef and any accumulated juices to wok; heat through. Serve over noodles, if desired. Garnish, if desired.

Makes 4 servings

Beef Benihana

KOREAN BEEF

1 pound beef flank steak or boneless sirloin
¼ cup low sodium soy sauce
2 tablespoons sugar
1 tablespoon sesame oil
1 teaspoon ground ginger
¼ teaspoon crushed red pepper
¼ small head napa cabbage

3 tablespoons vegetable oil, divided
1 can (14½ ounces) beef broth
1 cup packaged peeled baby carrots
2 cups frozen cauliflowerettes, thawed
1 cup frozen green bean cuts, thawed
Hot cooked rice noodles or rice

• Slice beef across prominent grain into ¼-inch-thick slices. Combine soy sauce, sugar, sesame oil, ginger and red pepper in large bowl. Add beef and toss to mix well. Set aside.

• Cut cabbage crosswise into 1-inch slices. Set aside.

• Heat wok over high heat about 1 minute or until hot. Drizzle 1½ tablespoons vegetable oil into wok and heat 30 seconds.

• Drain beef; reserve marinade. Add half of beef to wok; stir-fry until well browned. Remove to large bowl. Repeat with remaining 1½ tablespoons vegetable oil and beef.

• Add reserved marinade and broth to wok; cover wok and heat to a boil. Add carrots; cook, uncovered, about 5 minutes or until crisp-tender. Add cabbage, cauliflowerettes and green beans; cook and stir until tender. Return beef and any accumulated juices to wok and heat through. Serve over noodles in soup bowls. *Makes 4 servings*

MOUSSAKA–STYLE BEEF AND ZUCCHINI

3 medium zucchini
1 tablespoon vegetable oil
1 pound lean ground beef or chuck
1 medium onion, chopped
2 cloves garlic, minced
1 teaspoon dried basil leaves, crushed

½ teaspoon ground cinnamon
2 cans (8 ounces each) tomato sauce
½ cup low fat or nonfat sour cream
1 large egg yolk
¼ cup feta cheese
Hot cooked orzo (optional)

• Cut each zucchini crosswise into thirds. Cut pieces lengthwise into slices.

• Heat wok over high heat about 1 minute or until hot. Drizzle oil into wok and heat 30 seconds. Add zucchini and stir-fry 8 minutes. Remove zucchini to medium bowl.

• Add beef to wok and stir-fry until well browned. Add onion and garlic; stir-fry 1 minute. Reduce heat to medium. Add basil and cinnamon; mix well. Stir in tomato sauce; cover wok and simmer 5 minutes. Mix sour cream and egg yolk in small bowl until well blended.

• Skim off excess fat from beef mixture. Spread beef mixture to an even layer. Arrange zucchini in single layer over beef mixture. Spoon sour cream mixture in center of zucchini. Cover; cook 5 minutes or until top is set. Sprinkle with cheese. Remove from heat; let stand 1 minute. Serve with orzo, if desired. *Makes 4 servings*

Korean Beef

HUNAN CHILI BEEF

1 pound beef flank steak
3 tablespoons low sodium soy
    sauce
3 tablespoons vegetable oil, divided
1 tablespoon rice wine *or* dry sherry
1 tablespoon cornstarch
2 teaspoons brown sugar
1 jalapeño pepper, stemmed, seeded

3 green onions with tops
¼ small red bell pepper
1 small piece fresh ginger
    (1 inch long), minced
2 cloves garlic, minced
1 cup baby corn
1 teaspoon hot chili oil
Hot cooked rice

• Cut beef into 2 × ¼-inch-thick slices. Combine soy sauce, 1 tablespoon vegetable oil, wine, cornstarch and sugar in large bowl. Add beef; set aside. Cut jalapeño lengthwise into strips. Cut onions into 1-inch pieces. Cut red pepper lengthwise into ¼-inch strips.

• Heat wok over high heat 1 minute. Drizzle 1 tablespoon vegetable oil into wok; heat 30 seconds. Add half of beef mixture. Stir-fry until well browned. Remove to large bowl. Repeat with remaining 1 tablespoon vegetable oil and beef mixture. Reduce heat to medium. Add ginger, garlic, onions and corn to wok; stir-fry 1 minute. Add jalapeño and red pepper; stir-fry 1 minute.

• Return beef and any accumulated juices to wok; add chili oil. Toss to combine; heat through. Serve with rice. *Makes 4 servings*

VEGETABLE BEEF LO MEIN

3 packages (3 ounces each) beef
    flavor instant ramen noodles
4 cups boiling water
1 pound beef flank steak
2 green onions with tops
12 ounces bok choy
1 small red bell pepper

1 cup beef broth
¼ cup teriyaki sauce
1 tablespoon cornstarch
2 tablespoons vegetable oil
1 can (8 ounces) sliced bamboo
    shoots, drained

• Place noodles in large heat-proof bowl; add water. Let stand 10 minutes; drain.

• Cut beef into 2 × ¼-inch slices. Cut onions into 1-inch pieces. Separate bok choy leaves from stems; rinse and pat dry. Cut leaves crosswise into 1-inch slices. Cut stems diagonally into ¼-inch slices. Cut red pepper lengthwise into thin slices. Set aside. Combine broth, teriyaki and cornstarch in small bowl; stir until smooth.

• Heat wok over high heat about 1 minute or until hot. Drizzle oil into wok; heat 30 seconds. Add beef and stir-fry until well browned. Remove beef to large bowl. Add bok choy stems; stir-fry 1 minute. Stir in bok choy leaves and bamboo shoots; stir-fry 1 minute. Stir cornstarch mixture until smooth; add to wok. Cook until sauce boils and thickens. Stir in pepper and onions and heat 1 minute. Reduce heat to medium.

• Return beef and any accumulated juices to wok. Add noodles and mix gently with beef and vegetables; heat through. Transfer to serving dish. *Makes 4 servings*

Hunan Chili Beef

FIVE-SPICE BEEF AND BOK CHOY

1 boneless beef sirloin steak
　　(about 1 pound)
¼ cup soy sauce
2 tablespoons dry sherry
2 teaspoons minced fresh ginger
2 cloves garlic, minced
1 teaspoon sugar
½ teaspoon Chinese five-spice powder

¼ teaspoon crushed red pepper
　　(optional)
1 large head bok choy
2 teaspoons cornstarch
2 tablespoons peanut oil or vegetable
　　oil, divided
Hot cooked Chinese egg noodles
Thai red chili peppers for garnish

•Cut beef across prominent grain into ⅛-inch-thick slices; cut each slice into 2-inch pieces. Combine soy sauce, sherry, ginger, garlic, sugar, five-spice powder and red pepper in large bowl. Toss beef with soy sauce mixture. Set aside.

•Separate bok choy leaves from stems; rinse and pat dry. Stack leaves and cut into 1-inch slices. Cut stems diagonally into ½-inch slices.

•Drain beef; reserve marinade. Combine reserved marinade and cornstarch in small bowl; stir until smooth. Set aside.

•Heat wok over medium-high heat until hot. Drizzle 1 tablespoon oil into wok and heat 30 seconds. Add beef; stir-fry 2 minutes or until beef is barely pink in center. Remove beef to large bowl.

•Add remaining 1 tablespoon oil. Add bok choy stems; stir-fry 3 minutes. Add bok choy leaves; stir-fry 2 minutes.

•Stir marinade mixture until smooth; add to wok. Stir-fry 1 minute or until sauce boils and thickens.

•Return beef and any accumulated juices to wok; heat through. Serve over noodles. Garnish, if desired.

Makes 4 servings

❧❀❧

*F*ive-spice powder is a cocoa-colored blend of five ground spices, usually anise seed, fennel, clove, cinnamon and ginger or pepper. It has a slightly sweet, pungent flavor and should be used sparingly.

Five-Spice Beef and Bok Choy

MANDARIN TOMATO BEEF

1 boneless beef sirloin steak, cut
   1 inch thick (about 1 pound)
½ cup low sodium teriyaki sauce
2 teaspoons minced fresh ginger
2 teaspoons cornstarch
2 tablespoons peanut oil or vegetable
   oil, divided
1 medium onion, cut into ½-inch
   wedges

2 cups fresh snow peas *or* 1 package
   (6 ounces) frozen snow peas,
   thawed
2 medium tomatoes, cut into ½-inch
   wedges
   Hot cooked rice
   Freshly ground black pepper
   (optional)

• Cut beef across prominent grain into ⅛-inch-thick slices; cut each slice into 2-inch pieces. Combine teriyaki and ginger in large bowl. Toss beef with teriyaki mixture. Marinate beef 10 minutes.

• Drain beef; reserve marinade. Combine reserved marinade and cornstarch in small bowl; stir until smooth. Set aside.

• Heat wok over medium-high heat until hot. Drizzle 1 tablespoon oil into wok and heat 30 seconds. Add half of beef; stir-fry 2 to 3 minutes or until beef is barely pink in center. Remove beef to large bowl. Repeat with remaining beef.

• Drizzle remaining 1 tablespoon oil into wok. Add onion; cook 3 minutes or until browned, stirring occasionally. Add snow peas; stir-fry 3 minutes for fresh snow peas (or 1 minute for frozen snow peas).

• Stir reserved marinade until smooth and add to wok. Stir-fry 30 seconds or until sauce boils and thickens.

• Return beef, any accumulated juices and tomatoes to wok; heat through. Serve over rice. Sprinkle with pepper, if desired.

Makes 4 servings

❦

Snow peas, also called Chinese peas, are flat, green pods that are picked before the peas have matured. They add crispness, color and flavor to this delicious dish.

Mandarin Tomato Beef

MOO SHU BEEF

½ pound deli roast beef, cut ⅛ inch thick
1 tablespoon dry sherry
3 teaspoons low sodium soy sauce, divided
2 teaspoons cornstarch, divided
1 teaspoon minced fresh ginger
1 clove garlic, minced
½ teaspoon sugar
¼ cup beef broth
¼ cup water
3 tablespoons peanut oil or vegetable oil, divided

1 egg, slightly beaten
1 cup shredded carrots
3 green onions with tops, cut into ½-inch pieces
1 can (8 ounces) sliced bamboo shoots, drained, cut into thin strips
Hoisin or plum sauce
8 flour tortillas (7 to 8 inches), warmed

• Cut beef into thin strips. Combine sherry, 1 teaspoon soy sauce, 1 teaspoon cornstarch, ginger, garlic and sugar in large bowl; stir until smooth. Add beef to sherry mixture; toss to coat. Marinate 10 minutes.

• Stir broth, water and remaining 2 teaspoons soy sauce into remaining 1 teaspoon cornstarch in cup until smooth.

• Heat wok over high heat about 1 minute or until hot. Drizzle 1 tablespoon oil into wok. Pour egg into wok; tilt to coat bottom. Scramble egg, breaking into small pieces as it cooks. Remove from wok; set aside.

• Add remaining 2 tablespoons oil to wok. Add carrots; stir-fry 1 minute (carrots will still be crisp-tender). Add beef mixture, onions and bamboo shoots; stir-fry 1 minute. Stir broth mixture until smooth; add to wok. Stir-fry 1 minute or until sauce boils and thickens. Cook 1 minute more. Stir in egg.

• Spread hoisin sauce on each tortilla. Spoon beef mixture over sauce. Fold bottom of tortilla up over filling, then fold sides over filling. Transfer to serving plate.

Makes 4 servings

*H*oisin sauce is a thick, dark brown sauce made from soybeans, flour, sugar, spices, garlic, chili and salt. It has a sweet, spicy flavor.

SPICY BEEF STIR–FRY

5 tablespoons low sodium teriyaki sauce, divided
1 teaspoon hot chili oil *or* ½ teaspoon crushed Szechuan peppercorns
1 boneless beef sirloin, top loin or tenderloin steak, cut 1 inch thick (about 1 pound)
1 tablespoon dry sherry
1 tablespoon cornstarch

2 tablespoons peanut oil or vegetable oil, divided
2 cups sliced mushrooms
1 small onion, cut into 1-inch pieces
Hot cooked angel hair pasta
Thinly sliced green onions and red and yellow bell pepper pieces for garnish

•Combine 1 tablespoon teriyaki and chili oil in large bowl. Cut beef across prominent grain into ⅛-inch-thick slices; cut each slice into 1½-inch pieces. Toss beef with teriyaki mixture.

•Combine remaining 4 tablespoons teriyaki, sherry and cornstarch in small bowl; stir until smooth.

•Heat wok over high heat about 1 minute or until hot. Drizzle 1 tablespoon peanut oil into wok and heat 30 seconds. Add half of beef mixture; stir-fry 2 minutes or until beef is barely pink in center. Remove beef to large bowl. Repeat with remaining beef mixture. Reduce heat to medium-high.

•Heat remaining 1 tablespoon peanut oil in wok. Add mushrooms and onion; stir-fry 5 minutes or until vegetables are tender.

•Stir teriyaki mixture until smooth and add to wok. Stir-fry 30 seconds or until sauce boils and thickens.

•Return beef and any accumulated juices to wok; heat through. Serve over pasta. Garnish, if desired.

Makes 4 servings

*H*ot chili oil is a reddish-colored, fiery hot oil made from peanut oil infused with dried red chili peppers. It is also called chili pepper oil or hot pepper oil.

Spicy Beef Stir-Fry

FAST-FIXIN' PORK

SWEET AND SOUR PORK

1 pound boneless pork loin
1 medium onion
1 medium green bell pepper,
   stemmed and seeded
2 medium ripe peaches
1 can (8 ounces) pineapple chunks
   packed in juice

¼ cup distilled white vinegar
3 tablespoons light brown sugar
1 tablespoon cornstarch
1 tablespoon soy sauce
2 tablespoons vegetable oil
   Hot cooked rice

• Trim fat from pork; discard. Cut pork into 1-inch cubes. Cut onion into 8 wedges. Cut pepper into 1-inch pieces. Cut peaches in half; discard pits. Cut each peach half into 6 wedges. Set aside.

• Drain pineapple, reserving juice in cup. Add vinegar, sugar, cornstarch and soy sauce to pineapple juice; stir until smooth. Set aside.

• Heat wok over medium-high heat until hot. Drizzle oil into wok and heat 30 seconds. Add pork and stir-fry about 7 minutes or until well browned. Add onion and stir-fry 2 minutes or until onion is tender. Stir in pepper and stir-fry 1 minute. Reduce heat to medium.

• Stir cornstarch mixture until smooth; add to wok. Add peaches and pineapple; cook and stir until sauce boils and thickens. Transfer to serving dish. Serve with rice.

Makes 4 servings

PAPRIKA PORK WITH SPINACH

1 pound boneless pork loin or leg
3 tablespoons all-purpose flour
3 tablespoons vegetable oil
1 cup frozen pearl onions, thawed
1 tablespoon paprika
1 can (14½ ounces) vegetable or
  chicken broth

8 ounces medium curly egg noodles,
  uncooked
1 package (10 ounces) frozen leaf
  spinach, thawed and well drained
½ cup sour cream
  Fresh spinach leaves and red bell
  pepper strips for garnish

• Trim fat from pork; discard. Cut pork into 1-inch cubes. Place flour and pork in resealable plastic food storage bag; shake until well coated.

• Heat wok over high heat about 1 minute or until hot. Drizzle oil into wok and heat 30 seconds. Add pork and stir-fry about 5 minutes or until well browned on all sides. Remove pork to large bowl.

• Add onions and paprika to wok. Stir-fry 1 minute. Stir in broth, noodles and pork. Cover wok and bring to a boil. Reduce heat to low and cook, stirring occasionally, about 8 minutes or until noodles and pork are tender.

• Stir spinach into pork and noodles. Cover wok and cook until heated through. Add additional broth or water if needed. Add sour cream; mix well. Transfer to serving dish. Garnish, if desired.   *Makes 4 servings*

*P*aprika is used frequently as a seasoning and garnish for a variety of dishes. Its color ranges from orange-red to deep red with flavor ranging from mild to pungent.

Paprika Pork with Spinach

ORIENTAL–STYLE GROUND PORK

1 package (8 ounces) shredded
  carrots
1 tablespoon sugar
1 teaspoon distilled white vinegar or
  rice vinegar
2 green onions with tops
8 large mushrooms

¼ cup chicken broth
1 tablespoon low sodium soy sauce
1 teaspoon cornstarch
½ teaspoon chili powder
1 tablespoon vegetable oil
1 pound ground pork
  Boston lettuce leaves

• Combine carrots, sugar and vinegar in medium bowl; set aside.

• Slice onions diagonally into 1-inch pieces. Rinse mushrooms and pat dry with paper towels. Slice mushrooms. Combine broth, soy sauce, cornstarch and chili powder in small bowl; stir until smooth.

• Heat wok over medium-high heat until hot. Drizzle oil into wok and heat 30 seconds. Add pork and stir-fry until well browned. Add mushrooms and stir-fry until tender. Stir cornstarch mixture until smooth and add to pork. Cook until sauce boils and thickens. Stir in onions and stir-fry 1 minute.

• Line serving plate with lettuce leaves. Arrange carrot mixture in layer over leaves. Top with pork mixture. (Traditionally, the lettuce leaves are eaten as a wrapper to hold the ground meat mixture.)   *Makes 4 servings*

Look for firm, fleshy mushrooms with no discoloration or bruises. To store, keep refrigerated, unwashed, in a paper bag, ventilated package or a plastic bag punched with holes up to 5 days. If damp, wrap mushrooms in paper towels before storing. Use as soon as possible for best flavor.

Oriental-Style Ground Pork

PORK SATAY

1 pound boneless pork loin
3 tablespoons low sodium soy sauce, divided
½ teaspoon curry powder
½ cup creamy peanut butter
2 tablespoons brown sugar
2 tablespoons lime or lemon juice
1 tablespoon sesame oil

⅔ cup water
2 medium cucumbers
½ small red onion
2 tablespoons granulated sugar
2 tablespoons distilled white vinegar
½ teaspoon salt
2 tablespoons vegetable oil

• Cut pork horizontally in half to split the loin; cut each half crosswise into ¼-inch-thick slices. Combine pork, 1 tablespoon soy sauce and curry powder in large bowl. Set aside.

• Combine peanut butter, brown sugar, remaining 2 tablespoons soy sauce, lime juice and sesame oil in small bowl until blended. Gradually stir in water until smooth. Set aside.

• Peel cucumbers and cut lengthwise in half. Scoop out seeds. Slice cucumbers into thin slices. Thinly slice onion. Combine cucumbers, onion, granulated sugar, vinegar and salt in large bowl. Set aside.

• Heat wok over high heat about 1 minute or until hot. Drizzle vegetable oil into wok and heat 30 seconds. Add pork mixture and stir-fry until well browned on both sides. Reduce heat to medium.

• Add peanut butter mixture to wok and heat through. Transfer pork to serving platter. Spoon cucumber mixture around pork.   *Makes 4 servings*

EGG FOO YUNG

8 ounces fully cooked smoked ham steak, cut ½ inch thick
1 rib celery
1 can (8 ounces) whole water chestnuts, drained
1 green onion with tops
1 cup ⅓-less-salt chicken broth

1 tablespoon cornstarch
1 teaspoon soy sauce
¼ teaspoon ground ginger
¼ teaspoon sugar
6 tablespoons vegetable oil, divided
4 large eggs

• Cut ham into ¼-inch strips; cut strips crosswise into ¼-inch pieces. Slice celery. Coarsely chop water chestnuts and onion. Set aside.

• Combine broth, cornstarch, soy sauce, ginger and sugar in small bowl; stir until smooth. Set aside.

•Heat wok over medium-high heat 1 minute. Drizzle 1 tablespoon oil into wok and heat 30 seconds. Add ham, celery, water chestnuts and onion; stir-fry about 2 minutes or until ham is lightly browned. Remove ham mixture to medium bowl. Beat eggs into ham mixture until well mixed.

•Heat wok over medium-high heat 1 minute. Drizzle 1 tablespoon oil into wok and heat 30 seconds. Ladle about 1/4 cup egg mixture into wok and fry until underside is set and lightly browned. Turn egg foo yung over and fry other side just until set. Move fried egg foo yung to one side of wok. Repeat with remaining egg mixture, adding more oil as needed.

•Transfer egg foo yung to serving plate and keep warm. Stir cornstarch mixture until smooth and pour into wok. Cook and stir until sauce boils and thickens. Spoon sauce over egg foo yung. *Makes 4 servings*

CREOLE FRIED RICE AND BEANS

8 ounces kielbasa
1 large onion
1 rib celery
3 tablespoons vegetable oil
4 ounces green beans, cut into
    1-inch pieces
2 cloves garlic, chopped
1/2 cup water
4 cups cooked long-grain white rice,
    cooled

1/4 cup tomato sauce
1/2 teaspoon salt
1/2 teaspoon dried thyme leaves,
    crushed
1/4 teaspoon hot pepper sauce
1 cup canned red kidney beans,
    drained and rinsed

•Cut kielbasa into 1/2-inch-thick slices. Chop onion. Cut celery into slices.

•Heat wok over medium-low heat 1 minute. Drizzle oil into wok and heat 30 seconds. Add onion and celery; stir-fry 3 minutes. Add kielbasa, green beans and garlic; stir-fry 5 minutes. Add water; cover wok and cook until beans are crisp-tender.

•Add rice, tomato sauce, salt, thyme and hot pepper sauce to wok. Stir-fry until rice is well mixed and heated through. Add kidney beans and stir-fry until heated through. Transfer to serving dish. *Makes 4 to 6 servings*

*K*ielbasa, a garlic-flavored sausage, is made from seasoned pork, beef and veal.

ASIAN GINGER GLAZED PORK

1 pound pork tenderloin
2 tablespoons cornstarch
4 green onions with tops
1 piece fresh ginger (1 inch long)
2 cloves garlic
3 tablespoons vegetable oil, divided
¼ cup dry sherry
1 tablespoon soy sauce
1 to 2 tablespoons water
2 teaspoons brown sugar
¼ teaspoon crushed red pepper
¼ cup unsalted roasted cashews,
    chopped
Hot cooked rice
Fresh herb sprigs and bell pepper
    triangles for garnish

• Trim fat from pork; discard. Cut pork crosswise into ¼-inch-thick slices. Place cornstarch on waxed paper. Coat both sides of pork with cornstarch. Reserve remaining cornstarch. Set aside.

• Cut onions into 1-inch pieces. Thinly slice ginger. Stack ginger, a few slices at a time, and cut into fine strips. Finely chop garlic. Set aside.

• Heat wok over high heat about 1 minute or until hot. Drizzle 1 tablespoon oil into wok and heat 30 seconds. Add half of pork and stir-fry until well browned on both sides. Remove pork to plate. Repeat with 1 tablespoon oil and remaining pork. Reduce heat to medium.

• Add remaining 1 tablespoon oil, ginger, garlic and onions to wok; stir-fry 1 minute. Stir in reserved cornstarch. Add sherry, soy sauce, 1 tablespoon water, sugar and red pepper. Cook and stir until sauce boils and thickens. Stir in additional water if needed.

• Spoon sauce over pork until coated and glazed. Sprinkle with cashews. Serve with rice. Garnish, if desired.

Makes 4 servings

Cashews, kidney-shaped nuts with a sweet, buttery flavor, add a nice crunch to this dish.

Asian Ginger Glazed Pork

NORMANDY PORK AND CABBAGE

1 pound boneless pork loin or
    tenderloin
2 medium red baking apples, cored
1 tablespoon vegetable oil
2 tablespoons butter, divided
1 package (8 ounces) shredded green
    cabbage for coleslaw *or* 2 cups
    shredded red cabbage
1 tablespoon all-purpose flour

1 teaspoon ground sage
½ teaspoon salt
¼ teaspoon black pepper
½ cup beef broth
½ cup apple juice or sweet apple
    cider
¼ cup heavy cream
    Hot cooked egg noodles
    Green onions for garnish

• Trim fat from pork; discard. Cut pork crosswise into ¼-inch-thick slices. Set aside. Cut each apple in half; cut each half into 6 wedges. Set aside.

• Heat wok over high heat about 1 minute or until hot. Drizzle oil into wok and heat 30 seconds. Add 1 tablespoon butter and swirl to coat bottom. Add half of pork and stir-fry until well browned on both sides. Remove pork to large bowl. Repeat with remaining pork. Reduce heat to medium.

• Add remaining 1 tablespoon butter and apples to wok; stir-fry about 2 minutes or just until apples soften. Remove apples to bowl with pork.

• Add cabbage to wok; stir-fry just until wilted. Sprinkle in flour, sage, salt and pepper; stir-fry until well mixed. Add broth and juice; cook and stir until sauce boils and thickens. Add cream and heat through. Return pork and apples to wok. Stir in additional broth or water if needed. Serve with noodles. Garnish, if desired.

Makes 4 servings

*F*or best results in this recipe, use Cortland, Rome Beauty, Winesap
or Arkansas Black apples. They will remain flavorful and firm
during cooking.

Normandy Pork and Cabbage

PINEAPPLE HAM FRIED RICE

8 ounces fully cooked smoked ham
   steak, cut ½ inch thick
1 small green bell pepper, stemmed
   and seeded
2 green onions with tops
3 tablespoons vegetable oil, divided
2 tablespoons sliced almonds
4 cups cooked long-grain white rice,
   cooled

1 can (5¼ ounces) pineapple
   chunks packed in juice
2 tablespoons dark raisins
2 to 3 tablespoons low sodium
   soy sauce
1 tablespoon sesame oil

• Cut ham into 2-inch strips. Cut pepper lengthwise into ¼-inch strips. Coarsely chop onions.

• Heat wok over medium-high heat 1 minute. Drizzle 1 tablespoon vegetable oil into wok and heat 30 seconds. Add almonds and stir-fry until golden brown. Remove to plate; set aside. Add remaining 2 tablespoons vegetable oil and stir-fry pepper, ham and onions 2 minutes. Add rice, pineapple with juice and raisins. Stir-fry rice mixture until heated through.

• Sprinkle rice mixture with soy sauce to taste. Add sesame oil; stir-fry until well mixed. Transfer to serving bowl. Sprinkle with almonds. *Makes 4 to 6 servings*

BARBECUED PORK

1 pound boneless pork loin
2 medium onions
1 medium green bell pepper,
   stemmed and seeded
2 cloves garlic
1 tablespoon vegetable oil

1 can (8 ounces) tomato sauce
¼ cup brown sugar
2 tablespoons hoisin sauce
1 to 2 tablespoons cider vinegar
½ teaspoon salt
   Toasted sesame seed buns (optional)

• Trim fat from pork; discard. Cut pork crosswise into ¼-inch-thick slices. Stack a few slices at a time and cut into ¼-inch-wide julienne strips. Cut onions in half and cut crosswise into slices. Cut pepper into ½-inch pieces. Finely chop garlic.

• Heat wok over high heat about 1 minute or until hot. Drizzle oil into wok and heat 30 seconds. Add pork and stir-fry until well browned. Reduce heat to medium.

• Add onions and garlic to pork; stir-fry 1 minute. Stir in tomato sauce, sugar, hoisin, vinegar and salt. Cover wok and cook 5 minutes, stirring occasionally. Stir in pepper and stir-fry until crisp-tender. Serve pork mixture over toasted buns, if desired. *Makes 4 servings*

Pineapple Ham Fried Rice

ASPARAGUS CHICKEN

1 pound chicken breast tenders	1 green onion with tops
1 large egg white	1 package (10 ounces) frozen
2 tablespoons cornstarch, divided	asparagus, partially thawed
2 teaspoons *plus* 1 tablespoon soy	1/2 cup 1/3-less-salt chicken broth
sauce, divided	1 teaspoon sesame oil
2 teaspoons dry sherry	3 tablespoons vegetable oil, divided
2 large carrots, peeled	Hot cooked rice

•Rinse chicken and pat dry with paper towels. Cut each chicken tender crosswise in half. Combine egg white, 1 tablespoon cornstarch, 2 teaspoons soy sauce and sherry in large bowl; stir until smooth. Add chicken and toss to coat. Set aside.

•Slice carrots crosswise into 2-inch pieces. Slice carrot pieces lengthwise; stack slices and cut lengthwise into julienne strips. Cut onion diagonally into 1/2-inch slices. Cut asparagus spears diagonally into 11/2-inch pieces. Set aside.

•Combine broth, remaining 1 tablespoon cornstarch, remaining 1 tablespoon soy sauce and sesame oil in cup; stir until smooth. Set aside.

•Heat wok over high heat about 1 minute or until hot. Drizzle 2 tablespoons vegetable oil into wok and heat 30 seconds. Add chicken mixture and stir-fry about 4 minutes or until chicken is no longer pink in center. Remove to medium bowl. Reduce heat to medium.

•Drizzle remaining 1 tablespoon vegetable oil into wok. Add carrots and stir-fry about 3 minutes or until crisp-tender. Add asparagus and stir-fry 1 minute. Stir cornstarch mixture until smooth and add to wok. Cook until sauce boils and thickens. Stir in onion, chicken and any accumulated juices to wok; heat through. Transfer to serving dish. Serve with rice.   *Makes 4 servings*

Asparagus Chicken

KUNG PAO CHICKEN

1 pound boneless skinless chicken
  breasts
1 tablespoon cornstarch
1 large egg white
1 small piece fresh ginger (1 inch
  long)
1 clove garlic
1 tablespoon dry sherry
1 tablespoon soy sauce
1 tablespoon sesame oil

1 teaspoon sugar
1/1 teaspoon crushed red pepper
1/4 teaspoon salt
1/4 cup vegetable oil
1 small green bell pepper, cut into
  1/2-inch pieces
2 green onions with tops, cut into
  11/2-inch pieces
1/3 cup unsalted dry roasted peanuts
  Hot cooked rice (optional)

•Rinse chicken and pat dry with paper towels. Cut chicken crosswise into 1/4-inch-thick slices. Combine chicken and cornstarch in large bowl. Add egg white; stir to combine. Set aside.

•Mince ginger and garlic.

•Combine sherry, soy sauce, sesame oil, sugar, red pepper and salt in cup. Set aside.

•Heat wok over high heat about 1 minute or until hot. Drizzle vegetable oil into wok and heat 30 seconds. Add chicken mixture and stir-fry until chicken is no longer pink in center. Remove chicken to large bowl. Reduce heat to medium.

•Add ginger and garlic to wok; stir-fry 30 seconds. Add green pepper and onions; stir-fry 1 minute. Return chicken to wok. Add peanuts and sherry mixture; stir-fry until well mixed and heated through. Transfer chicken mixture to serving dish. Serve with rice, if desired.

Makes 4 servings

❧❦❧

Kung Pao Chicken is a Szechuan specialty. This recipe uses crushed red pepper for heat and is milder than recipes using dried red chilies.

Kung Pao Chicken

CHICKEN THIGHS WITH PEAS

8 boneless skinless chicken thighs
2 tablespoons vegetable oil
2 tablespoons low sodium soy sauce
2 tablespoons dry sherry
1 teaspoon ground ginger
1 teaspoon sugar
1/4 teaspoon garlic powder
1/2 small head iceberg lettuce

1 cup 1/3-less-salt chicken broth
2 tablespoons cornstarch
1 package (10 ounces) frozen green
    peas, partially thawed
Hot cooked rice
Red onion, red cabbage and
    snow peas for garnish

• Rinse chicken and pat dry with paper towels. Cut chicken into 1-inch pieces.

• Heat wok over high heat about 1 minute or until hot. Drizzle oil into wok and heat 30 seconds. Add chicken and stir-fry about 4 minutes or until chicken is well browned and no longer pink in center. Reduce heat to low. Add soy sauce, sherry, ginger, sugar and garlic powder. Cover wok and cook 5 minutes.

• Cut lettuce into 1/2-inch-wide slices. Rinse, drain and pat dry. Combine broth and cornstarch in cup; stir until smooth.

• Increase heat to high. Stir peas into chicken mixture. Cover wok and cook about 2 minutes or until heated through. Stir cornstarch mixture until smooth. Stir into chicken mixture. Heat until sauce boils and thickens. Add lettuce and stir-fry until wilted. Transfer to serving dish. Serve with rice. Garnish, if desired.   *Makes 4 to 6 servings*

Green peas, also called English peas, have a delicious, sweet flavor and are rich in vitamins A and C, niacin and iron. They add a wonderful splash of color to this scrumptious dish.

Chicken Thighs with Peas

HONEY ORANGE TURKEY

1 pound boneless skinless turkey
    cutlets
1/2 teaspoon salt
1/4 teaspoon black pepper
2 tablespoons cornstarch
1/2 cup orange juice
2 tablespoons honey

1 tablespoon soy sauce
1/2 teaspoon ground ginger
2 tablespoons vegetable oil
1 tablespoon butter or margarine
  Hot cooked rice
  Orange and lime slices for garnish

•Rinse turkey and pat dry with paper towels. Cut into quarters. Place turkey on waxed paper and sprinkle with salt and pepper. Dust with cornstarch. Set aside turkey and any remaining cornstarch.

•Combine orange juice, honey, soy sauce and ginger in cup; stir until well blended. Set aside.

•Heat wok over high heat about 1 minute or until hot. Drizzle oil into wok and heat 30 seconds. Add butter and turkey. Stir-fry until turkey is lightly browned on all sides. Remove turkey to large plate. Reduce heat to medium.

•Add remaining cornstarch to wok and mix well. Add orange juice mixture and heat to a boil, stirring to loosen any browned bits. Boil sauce 1 minute. Pour sauce over turkey. Serve with rice. Garnish, if desired. *Makes 4 servings*

MALAY SPICED CHICKEN

1 pound boneless skinless chicken
    breasts
2 medium onions
4 cloves garlic
1 small piece fresh ginger (3/4 inch
    long)
  Peel of 1/2 lemon
1 teaspoon ground cumin
1 teaspoon ground nutmeg
1 teaspoon turmeric

1/2 teaspoon ground cinnamon
1/4 to 1/2 teaspoon ground red pepper
1/4 teaspoon ground cloves
3 tablespoons vegetable oil
2/3 cup water
2 tablespoons distilled white vinegar
1 tablespoon sugar
1/2 teaspoon salt
  Hot cooked rice
  Cilantro sprigs for garnish

•Rinse chicken and pat dry with paper towels. Cut chicken crosswise into 1/2-inch-wide strips. Chop onions, garlic and ginger. Finely grate lemon peel.

•Combine cumin, nutmeg, turmeric, cinnamon, red pepper and cloves in small bowl.

•Heat wok over medium heat until warm. Add spice mixture and stir-fry to release aroma and toast lightly. Return spice mixture to bowl. Increase heat to high.

•Drizzle oil into wok and heat 30 seconds. Add onions, garlic, ginger and lemon peel. Stir-fry about 5 minutes or until lightly browned. Add chicken and spice mixture. Stir-fry until chicken is no longer pink in center and is coated with spice mixture.

•Stir in water, vinegar, sugar and salt. Bring to a boil. Stir until half of liquid evaporates and mixture thickens slightly. Spoon chicken mixture over rice. Garnish, if desired. *Makes 4 servings*

Honey Orange Turkey

BANGKOK CHICKEN

1 pound boneless skinless chicken breasts
2 tablespoons chopped green onion
1 teaspoon anchovy paste *or* 1 canned anchovy fillet
3 cloves garlic, halved
1/4 teaspoon crushed red pepper
3 tablespoons vegetable oil
1 cup canned button mushrooms or straw mushrooms

1 cup baby corn
3 tablespoons low sodium soy sauce
2 teaspoons sugar
3/4 cup fresh basil leaves
    Boston or romaine lettuce leaves
    Red jalapeño or red Thai chili pepper flowers for garnish

•Rinse chicken and pat dry with paper towels. Cut chicken crosswise into 1/4-inch-wide slices.

•Combine onion, anchovy paste, garlic and crushed red pepper in food processor or blender; process until smooth. Set aside.

•Heat wok over high heat about 1 minute or until hot. Drizzle oil into wok and heat 30 seconds. Add chicken and stir-fry until chicken is no longer pink in center. Remove chicken to large bowl. Reduce heat to medium.

•Add onion mixture to wok and stir-fry 1 minute. Add mushrooms and corn; mix well. Add soy sauce and sugar; stir until sugar dissolves. Return chicken to wok. Stir-fry until heated through. Add basil; toss gently to combine.

•Line serving platter with lettuce leaves. Spoon chicken mixture onto lettuce. Garnish, if desired.

Makes 4 servings

*B*asil has a wonderful aroma and its flavor ranges from peppery and robust to sweet and spicy. Its color can be various shades of green or purple.

Bangkok Chicken

WALNUT CHICKEN

1 pound boneless skinless chicken
    thighs
1 tablespoon cornstarch
3 tablespoons soy sauce
1 tablespoon rice wine or dry sherry
2 tablespoons minced fresh ginger
2 cloves garlic, minced
¼ to ½ teaspoon crushed red pepper

3 tablespoons vegetable oil
½ cup walnut halves or pieces
½ cup sliced water chestnuts
1 cup frozen green bean cuts, thawed
2 green onions with tops, cut into
    1-inch pieces
¼ cup water
  Hot cooked rice

•Rinse chicken and pat dry with paper towels. Cut into 1-inch cubes.

•Combine cornstarch, soy sauce, rice wine, ginger, garlic and red pepper in large bowl; stir until smooth. Add chicken to cornstarch mixture; stir to combine. Marinate 10 minutes.

•Heat wok over high heat about 1 minute or until hot. Drizzle oil into wok and heat 30 seconds. Add walnuts; stir-fry about 1 minute or until lightly browned. Remove walnuts to small bowl; set aside.

•Add chicken mixture to wok; stir-fry about 5 to 7 minutes or until chicken is no longer pink in center. Add water chestnuts, green beans, onions and water, stirring to loosen any browned bits from bottom. Stir-fry until heated through. Serve over rice on serving dish. Sprinkle with walnuts.

Makes 4 servings

CHICKEN BALINESE

8 boneless skinless chicken thighs
¼ teaspoon salt
¼ teaspoon black pepper
1 small onion, coarsely chopped
2 cloves garlic
1 tablespoon chopped fresh ginger
8 unsalted roasted cashews

¼ teaspoon ground red pepper
3 tablespoons vegetable oil
½ cup ketchup
1 tablespoon brown sugar
1 tablespoon soy sauce
  Hot cooked rice
  Lime wedges for garnish

•Rinse chicken and pat dry with paper towels. Cut chicken crosswise into ¾-inch-wide strips. Place chicken on large plate and sprinkle with salt and black pepper.

•Combine onion, garlic, ginger, cashews and red pepper in food processor or blender; process until smooth paste forms, stopping occasionally to scrape side of container. Set aside.

•Heat wok over medium-high heat until hot. Drizzle oil into wok and heat 30 seconds. Add chicken and stir-fry about 4 minutes or until chicken is well browned and no longer pink in center. Reduce heat to medium.

•Spoon off all but 1 tablespoon oil from wok. Add onion mixture to chicken and gently stir-fry 2 minutes. Add ketchup, sugar and soy sauce. Stir until sugar dissolves. Spoon chicken mixture around rim of serving plate. Spoon rice into center. Garnish, if desired.

Makes 4 servings

Walnut Chicken

SWEET AND SOUR CHICKEN

6 ounces boneless skinless chicken
    breasts
2 tablespoons rice vinegar
2 tablespoons low sodium soy sauce
3 cloves garlic, minced
½ teaspoon minced fresh ginger
¼ teaspoon crushed red pepper
1 teaspoon vegetable oil
3 green onions with tops, cut into
    1-inch pieces

1 large green bell pepper, cut into
    1-inch squares
1 tablespoon cornstarch
½ cup ⅓-less-salt chicken broth
2 tablespoons apricot fruit spread
1 can (11 ounces) mandarin orange
    wedges
2 cups cooked white rice or Chinese
    egg noodles

• Rinse chicken and pat dry with paper towels. Cut chicken crosswise into ½-inch strips. Combine vinegar, soy sauce, garlic, ginger and red pepper in large bowl. Toss chicken with garlic mixture. Marinate 15 minutes.

• Heat wok over medium heat until hot. Drizzle oil into wok and heat 30 seconds. Drain chicken; reserve marinade. Add chicken to wok; stir-fry 3 minutes or until chicken is no longer pink in center. Stir in onions and green pepper; stir-fry 3 minutes or until vegetables are crisp-tender.

• Combine cornstarch and reserved marinade; stir until smooth.

• Stir broth, fruit spread and cornstarch mixture into wok. Stir-fry 1 minute or until sauce boils and thickens.

• Add orange wedges; heat through. Serve with rice.   *Makes 4 servings*

❧❦☙

The apricot fruit spread and mandarin oranges create the sweet and the vinegar creates the sour in this heavenly chicken stir-fry.

CHICKEN AND VEGETABLES WITH MUSTARD SAUCE

1 pound boneless skinless chicken breasts
1 tablespoon sugar
2 teaspoons cornstarch
2 teaspoons dry mustard
3 tablespoons low sodium soy sauce
2 tablespoons water
2 tablespoons rice vinegar
2 tablespoons vegetable oil, divided

2 cloves garlic, minced
1 small red bell pepper, cut into short thin strips
½ cup thinly sliced celery
1 small onion, cut into thin wedges
Chinese egg noodles
Fresh chives and yellow bell pepper rose for garnish

• Rinse chicken and pat dry with paper towels. Cut chicken into 1-inch pieces.

• Combine sugar, cornstarch and mustard in small bowl. Add soy sauce, water and vinegar to cornstarch mixture; stir until smooth. Set aside.

• Heat wok over medium heat until hot. Drizzle 1 tablespoon oil into wok and heat 30 seconds. Add chicken and garlic; stir-fry 5 to 6 minutes or until chicken is no longer pink in center. Remove chicken to large bowl.

• Drizzle remaining 1 tablespoon oil into wok. Add red pepper, celery and onion; stir-fry 3 minutes or until vegetables are crisp-tender.

• Stir soy sauce mixture; add to wok. Stir-fry 30 seconds or until sauce boils and thickens.

• Return chicken and any accumulated juices to wok; heat through. Serve with noodles. Garnish, if desired.

Makes 4 servings

*D**ry mustard is made from mustard seeds that are ground into a powder. It can be stored for about 6 months in a dry, dark place.*

Chicken and Vegetables with Mustard Sauce

STIR–FRIED CHICKEN WITH BROCCOLI

1 pound boneless skinless chicken tenders
2 tablespoons lemon juice
2 teaspoons grated lemon peel
1 teaspoon dried thyme leaves, crushed
½ teaspoon salt
¼ teaspoon ground white pepper
1 cup chicken broth
1 tablespoon cornstarch

3 tablespoons vegetable oil, divided
1 tablespoon butter
1 can (4 ounces) sliced, drained button mushrooms
1 medium red onion, peeled, sliced
1 can (14 ounces) pre-cut baby corn, rinsed and drained*
2 cups frozen broccoli cuts
Hot cooked rice

• Rinse chicken and pat dry with paper towels. Cut each chicken tender in half.

• Combine lemon juice, lemon peel, thyme, salt and pepper in large bowl. Add chicken to lemon mixture; coat well. Marinate 10 minutes.

• Combine broth and cornstarch in cup; stir until smooth. Set aside.

• Heat wok over medium-high heat until hot. Drizzle 1 tablespoon oil into wok. Add butter; swirl to coat bottom and heat until hot. Add mushrooms; stir-fry 1 minute. Add onion; stir-fry 2 minutes. Remove to large bowl.

• Heat remaining 2 tablespoons oil in wok. Stir-fry chicken in single layer 1½ minutes or until chicken is well browned on all sides and no longer pink in center. Remove to bowl with vegetable mixture.

• Add corn to wok and stir-fry about 1 minute. Stir cornstarch mixture until smooth; add to wok and cook until sauce boils and thickens. Add chicken mixture and broccoli to wok; stir-fry until heated through. Serve over rice.

Makes 4 to 6 servings

Or, substitute 15-ounce can whole baby corn, cut into 1-inch pieces.

❧❀❧

*B*aby corn are tender, miniature ears of corn that can be completely eaten, cob and all. They're also great in soups and salads.

Stir-Fried Chicken with Broccoli

CILANTRO–LIME CHICKEN

1 pound boneless skinless chicken
   breasts
2 small onions
1 to 2 small jalapeño peppers
1 small piece fresh ginger (1 inch
   long)
1 large lime

2 tablespoons vegetable oil
2 tablespoons chopped fresh cilantro
2 tablespoons low sodium soy sauce
1 to 2 teaspoons sugar
   Hot cooked rice
   Cilantro sprigs, lime zest and red
     chili pepper strips for garnish

•Rinse chicken and pat dry with paper towels. Cut each chicken breast half into 6 pieces. Cut each onion into 8 wedges. Cut jalapeño crosswise into slices. Cut ginger into thin slices.

•Remove 3 strips of peel from lime with vegetable peeler. Cut lime peel into very fine shreds. Juice lime; measure 2 tablespoons juice.

•Heat wok over medium-high heat until hot. Drizzle oil into wok and heat 30 seconds. Add chicken, jalapeño and ginger. Stir-fry about 3 minutes or until chicken is no longer pink in center. Reduce heat to medium.

•Add onions to wok; stir-fry 5 minutes.

•Add lime peel, lime juice and cilantro to chicken mixture; stir-fry 1 minute. Add soy sauce and sugar to taste; stir-fry until well mixed and heated through. Transfer to serving dish. Serve with rice. Garnish, if desired.

Makes 4 servings

❧❦❧

Cilantro is an herb that looks like flat leaf parsley, but its zesty flavor is unique. Cilantro can be found at many large supermarkets or at Mexican specialty food stores.

Cilantro-Lime Chicken

SEAFOOD IN A SNAP

STIR–FRIED SCALLOPS WITH VEGETABLES

1 pound sea scallops
¼ teaspoon salt
⅛ teaspoon black pepper
1 package (6 ounces) red radishes
½ cup vegetable broth
1 tablespoon cornstarch
3 tablespoons butter or margarine, divided

¼ cup dry white wine
1 package (6 ounces) frozen snow peas, partially thawed
½ cup sliced bamboo shoots
Hot cooked couscous

• Rinse scallops and pat dry with paper towels. Sprinkle with salt and pepper.

• Trim root and stem ends off radishes. Rinse radishes and pat dry with paper towels. Cut each radish into quarters; set aside.

• Combine broth and cornstarch in cup; stir until smooth. Set aside.

• Heat wok over high heat about 1 minute or until hot. Add 1½ tablespoons butter and swirl to coat bottom. Arrange half of scallops in single layer in wok, leaving ½ inch between (scallops should not touch). Cook scallops until browned on both sides. Remove scallops to large bowl. Repeat with remaining 1½ tablespoons butter and scallops. Reduce heat to medium-high.

• Add radishes to wok; stir-fry about 1 minute or until crisp-tender. Remove radishes to bowl with scallops.

• Add wine to wok. Stir cornstarch mixture; add to wok. Add snow peas and bamboo shoots; heat through.

• Return scallops and radishes to wok; stir-fry until heated through. Serve scallop mixture over couscous on serving plate.

Makes 4 servings

Stir-Fried Scallops with Vegetables

SHRIMP IN CHILI SAUCE

¾ **pound peeled and deveined large shrimp**
1 **tablespoon rice wine or dry sherry**
4 **cloves garlic, chopped**
1 **teaspoon paprika**
¼ **teaspoon crushed red pepper**
2 **tablespoons water**

2 **tablespoons ketchup**
1 **teaspoon cornstarch**
½ **teaspoon sugar**
¼ **teaspoon salt**
2 **tablespoons vegetable oil**
2 **tablespoons diced green chilies**

•Combine shrimp, wine, garlic, paprika and red pepper in medium bowl; mix well. Marinate 15 minutes.

•Combine water, ketchup, cornstarch, sugar and salt in small bowl; stir until smooth. Set aside.

•Heat wok over high heat about 1 minute or until hot. Drizzle oil into wok and heat 30 seconds. Add shrimp mixture and chilies; stir-fry about 3 minutes or until shrimp turn pink and opaque.

•Stir cornstarch mixture until smooth; add to wok. Cook and stir about 2 minutes or until sauce coats shrimp and thickens. Transfer shrimp mixture to serving dish or individual serving plates. *Makes 4 servings*

*G*reen chilies have a mild flavor with a slight bite. They are 4 to 6 inches long, about 1½ inches wide and have a rounded tip. Green chilies are also called Anaheims and are available fresh or canned.

Shrimp in Chili Sauce

SHRIMP IN MOCK LOBSTER SAUCE

½ cup ⅓-less-salt beef or chicken broth
¼ cup oyster sauce
1 tablespoon cornstarch
1 egg
1 egg white
1 tablespoon peanut oil or vegetable oil

¾ pound peeled and deveined medium or large shrimp
2 cloves garlic, minced
3 green onions with tops, cut into ½-inch pieces
Hot cooked Chinese egg noodles

• Combine broth, oyster sauce and cornstarch in small bowl; stir until smooth. Beat egg with egg white in separate small bowl. Set aside.

• Heat wok over medium-high heat until hot. Drizzle oil into wok and heat 30 seconds. Add shrimp and garlic; stir-fry 3 to 5 minutes or until shrimp turn pink and opaque.

• Stir broth mixture until smooth; add to wok. Add onions. Stir-fry 1 minute or until sauce boils and thickens.

• Stir eggs into wok. Stir-fry 1 minute or just until eggs are set. Serve over noodles.

Makes 4 servings

*O*yster sauce is a thick, brown, concentrated sauce made of ground oysters, soy sauce and brine. It imparts a slight fish flavor and is used as seasoning to intensify other flavors.

Shrimp in Mock Lobster Sauce

GINGERED FISH WITH BOK CHOY

1¼ pounds skinless mahi mahi fillets,
    cut 1 inch thick
2 tablespoons sake *or* dry sherry
½ teaspoon salt, divided
¼ teaspoon black pepper
1 piece fresh ginger (1 inch long)
1 pound bok choy
4 green onions with tops

2 cloves garlic
¼ cup teriyaki sauce
¼ cup water
1 tablespoon cornstarch
¼ cup vegetable oil, divided
    Hot cooked rice
    Bok choy and shredded red
      cabbage for garnish

• Rinse mahi mahi and pat dry with paper towels. Cut fish into 1¼-inch pieces. Combine fish, sake, ¼ teaspoon salt and pepper in large bowl. Set aside.

• Peel ginger and slice thinly; cut slices into very fine julienne strips. Separate bok choy into individual leaves. Rinse well and pat dry with paper towels. Cut bok choy stems diagonally into ½-inch slices. Cut leaves crosswise into 1-inch slices. Set bok choy stems in separate pile from leaves.

• Cut onions into 1-inch pieces. Finely chop garlic. Combine teriyaki, water and cornstarch in cup; stir until smooth. Set aside.

• Heat wok over high heat about 1 minute or until hot. Drizzle 1 tablespoon oil into wok and heat 30 seconds. Add bok choy stems and stir-fry about 2 minutes or until crisp-tender. Add bok choy leaves and garlic; stir-fry until tender. Sprinkle with remaining ¼ teaspoon salt. Transfer to serving plate; cover and keep warm.

• Drizzle remaining 3 tablespoons oil into wok and heat 30 seconds. Add fish and stir-fry gently about 4 minutes or until fish is lightly browned and flakes easily when tested with fork. Place fish over bok choy.

• Add onions and ginger to wok. Stir cornstarch mixture until smooth and add to wok. Stir-fry until sauce boils and thickens. Spoon sauce over fish. Serve with rice. Garnish, if desired.

Makes 4 servings

*B*ok choy, also known as Chinese cabbage, has long, white stalks and deep green, crinkled leaves. Bok choy has a sweet and mild cabbagelike flavor. Choose bok choy with fresh crisp leaves and firm stalks.

Gingered Fish with Bok Choy

PAD THAI (THAI FRIED NOODLES)

12 ounces dried thin rice stick noodles
4 tablespoons vegetable oil, divided
1¼ cups water
3 tablespoons brown sugar
¼ cup soy sauce
2 tablespoons lime juice
1 tablespoon anchovy paste
2 eggs, lightly beaten
12 ounces peeled and deveined
    medium shrimp
2 cloves garlic, minced

1 tablespoon paprika
¼ to ½ teaspoon crushed red pepper
1 cup canned bean sprouts, rinsed
    and drained, divided
½ cup coarsely chopped unsalted dry
    roasted peanuts
4 green onions with tops, cut into
    1-inch pieces
½ lime, cut lengthwise into 4 wedges
    for garnish

•Place 6 cups water in wok; bring to a boil over high heat. Add noodles; cook 2 minutes or until tender but still firm, stirring frequently. Drain; rinse under cold running water to stop cooking. Drain again and place noodles in large bowl. Add 1 tablespoon oil; toss lightly to coat. Set aside.

•Combine 1¼ cups water, sugar, soy sauce, lime juice and anchovy paste in small bowl; set aside.

•Heat wok over medium heat until hot. Drizzle 1 tablespoon oil into wok and heat 30 seconds. Add eggs; stir-fry 1 minute or just until set on bottom. Turn eggs over using flat spatula; stir to scramble. Remove to medium bowl; set aside. Increase heat to high.

•Drizzle 1 tablespoon oil into wok. Add shrimp and garlic; stir-fry 2 minutes or until shrimp begin to turn pink and opaque. Remove shrimp to bowl with eggs. Reduce heat to medium.

•Drizzle remaining 1 tablespoon oil into wok and heat 15 seconds. Stir in paprika and red pepper. Add noodles and anchovy mixture; cook and stir about 5 minutes or until noodles are softened. Stir in ¾ cup bean sprouts. Add peanuts and onions; toss and cook about 1 minute or until onions are tender. Add eggs and shrimp; stir-fry until heated through. Transfer to serving plate and garnish with remaining bean sprouts and lime wedges.

Makes 4 servings

❧✿❧

If rice stick noodles are unavailable, use fine egg noodles, thin spaghetti, vermicelli or angel hair pasta.

Pad Thai

THAI SEAFOOD STIR–FRY

1 tablespoon cornstarch
1 tablespoon low sodium soy sauce
2 tablespoons lemon juice
2 teaspoons sugar
½ teaspoon ground ginger
¼ teaspoon crushed red pepper
8 ounces broccoli
2 ribs celery

1 large onion
3 tablespoons vegetable oil
¼ cup water
1 pound surimi seafood chunks *or* imitation crab, thawed if frozen
½ cup sliced water chestnuts
Hot cooked rice

•Combine cornstarch, soy sauce, lemon juice, sugar, ginger and crushed red pepper in small bowl; stir until smooth. Set aside.

•Remove woody stems from broccoli; discard. Rinse flowerettes and cut into small pieces; set aside. Cut celery diagonally into ½-inch slices. Cut onion lengthwise in half; cut crosswise into slices.

•Heat wok over high heat about 1 minute or until hot. Drizzle oil into wok and heat 30 seconds. Add onion and stir-fry 1 minute. Add broccoli and celery; stir-fry 2 minutes. Reduce heat to medium-high. Add water; cover wok and cook until vegetables are crisp-tender. Add surimi and water chestnuts; stir-fry gently 1 minute to combine.

•Stir cornstarch mixture until smooth. Add to wok and stir-fry until sauce boils and thickens. Spoon into serving dish. Serve with rice.   *Makes 4 servings*

*S*urimi *seafood is processed fish, typically pollack, that is flavored and restructured to make seafood products. It comes in flakes, chunks, sticks or nuggets. This convenient seafood product is wonderful for creating quick, delicious meals such as this one.*

Thai Seafood Stir-Fry

MALABAR SHRIMP

4 green onions with tops
1 tablespoon vegetable oil
2 tablespoons butter or margarine
1 pound shelled and deveined
   medium shrimp
1 tablespoon curry powder
½ teaspoon grated lemon peel
½ teaspoon salt
½ teaspoon sugar
2 cloves garlic, minced

½ cup heavy cream
¼ cup diced mild green chilies
   Cooked bulgur
3 tablespoons coarsely chopped
   unsalted dry roasted peanuts
Toasted coconut *or* bottled
   chutney (optional)
Enoki mushrooms and red bell
   pepper strips for garnish

•Cut onions diagonally into 1-inch pieces.

•Heat wok over high heat about 1 minute or until hot. Drizzle oil into wok and heat 30 seconds. Add onions and stir-fry about 1 minute or until crisp-tender. Remove to small bowl.

•Add butter to wok and swirl to coat bottom. Add shrimp, curry powder, lemon peel, salt, sugar and garlic. Stir-fry about 3 minutes or until shrimp turn pink and opaque. Add cream and chilies and heat through. Return onions to wok.

•Serve shrimp mixture over bulgur. Sprinkle with peanuts and coconut, if desired. Garnish, if desired.

Makes 4 servings

❧❀❧

*T*o toast coconut, preheat oven to 300°F. Spread coconut on baking sheet and bake 4 to 6 minutes or until light golden brown, stirring frequently.

Malabar Shrimp

CREAMY SALMON WITH GREEN BEANS

1 large red salmon steak (about
 ¾ pound)
1 large ripe tomato
1 small onion
2 tablespoons butter or margarine
2 tablespoons all-purpose flour
1 cup vegetable or chicken broth
1 package (9 ounces) frozen green
 bean cuts, partially thawed

1 cup half-and-half
¼ teaspoon salt
¼ teaspoon ground white pepper
5 tablespoons grated Parmesan
 cheese, divided
Hot cooked angel hair pasta
Zucchini slices and red bell
 pepper strips for garnish

•Rinse salmon and pat dry with paper towels. Remove skin and bones; discard. Cut into ¾-inch pieces. Cut tomato into ½-inch pieces. Coarsely chop onion. Set aside.

•Heat wok over medium-high heat until hot. Add butter and swirl to coat bottom. Add salmon and stir-fry gently 3 to 4 minutes or until fish flakes easily when tested with fork. Remove to large bowl; cover and keep warm.

•Add tomato and onion; stir-fry about 5 minutes or until onion is tender. Stir in flour until well mixed. Increase heat to high. Stir in broth and green beans; stir-fry until sauce boils and thickens. Add salmon, half-and-half, salt and pepper. Stir-fry until heated through. Add half of cheese to salmon mixture; toss until well mixed. Spoon salmon mixture over pasta. Sprinkle with remaining cheese. Garnish, if desired.

Makes 4 servings

❧⚜❧

*T*here are several types of salmon available, but red salmon has a
firm-textured flesh making it ideal for this dish.

*Creamy Salmon with
Green Beans*

SHRIMP JAVA

1 pound shelled and deveined large
   shrimp
¼ cup low sodium soy sauce
2 tablespoons lime juice
1 tablespoon brown sugar
1 teaspoon ground cumin

½ teaspoon chili powder
2 cloves garlic, minced
½ small bunch fresh cilantro
3 tablespoons vegetable oil
   Hot cooked rice

• Combine shrimp, soy sauce, lime juice, sugar, cumin, chili powder and garlic in large bowl; stir until well mixed. Marinate 15 minutes.

• Remove and discard large stems from cilantro. Rinse cilantro in bowl of water several times to remove sand. Drain cilantro and dry in salad spinner. Coarsely chop cilantro.

• Heat wok over high heat about 1 minute or until hot. Drizzle oil into wok and heat 30 seconds. Add shrimp mixture. Stir-fry about 4 minutes or until shrimp turn pink and opaque. Add half of cilantro; toss to combine. Transfer to serving dish. Garnish with remaining cilantro. Serve with rice.   *Makes 4 servings*

NOODLES WITH BABY SHRIMP

1 package (3.75 ounces) bean thread
   noodles
3 green onions with tops
1 tablespoon vegetable oil
1 package (16 ounces) frozen mixed
   vegetables (such as cauliflower,
   broccoli and carrots), thawed

1 cup vegetable broth
8 ounces frozen baby shrimp
1 tablespoon soy sauce
2 teaspoons sesame oil
¼ teaspoon black pepper

• Place noodles in large bowl. Cover with hot tap water; let stand 10 to 15 minutes or just until softened. Drain noodles and cut into 5- or 6-inch pieces.

• Cut onions into 1-inch pieces.

• Heat wok over high heat about 1 minute or until hot. Drizzle vegetable oil into wok and heat 30 seconds. Add onions and stir-fry 1 minute. Add mixed vegetables and stir-fry 2 minutes. Add broth and heat to a boil. Reduce heat to low; cover wok and cook vegetables about 5 minutes or until crisp-tender.

• Add shrimp to vegetable mixture in wok and cook just until thawed. Stir in noodles, soy sauce, sesame oil and pepper; stir-fry until heated through. Transfer to serving dish.   *Makes 4 to 6 servings*

Shrimp Java

SHRIMP WITH PEANUTS

¼ cup ketchup
2 tablespoons ⅓-less-salt chicken
   broth
1 tablespoon dry sherry
1 tablespoon rice vinegar
1 tablespoon low sodium soy sauce
1 teaspoon brown sugar
2 large green onions with tops
2 cloves garlic

1 tablespoon peanut oil or vegetable
   oil
⅛ to ¼ teaspoon crushed red pepper
¾ pound peeled and deveined
   medium or large shrimp
⅓ cup dry roasted peanuts
   Hot cooked Chinese egg noodles
   Cucumber fan for garnish

•Combine ketchup, broth, sherry, vinegar, soy sauce and sugar in small bowl. Set aside.

•Cut onions diagonally into ½-inch pieces. Mince garlic.

•Heat wok over medium-high heat until hot. Drizzle oil into wok and heat 30 seconds. Add garlic and red pepper; stir-fry 30 seconds.

•Add shrimp to wok; stir-fry 3 to 5 minutes or until shrimp turn pink and opaque. Add ketchup mixture and onions. Stir-fry about 1 minute or until sauce boils and thickens.

•Stir in peanuts. Serve over noodles. Garnish, if desired.　　*Makes 4 servings*

*R*ice vinegar is a light, mellow and mildly tangy vinegar brewed from rice. Do not use brands that are not brewed or that are seasoned with salt and sugar. Cider vinegar can be used as a substitution for rice vinegar.

Shrimp with Peanuts

MEATLESS DISHES IN MINUTES

ℒℴ

STIR–FRIED BROCCOLI

1 pound broccoli
1 medium onion
2 ribs celery
4 ounces fresh bean sprouts
2 cloves garlic
1 tablespoon cornstarch
1 tablespoon cold water

1 tablespoon oyster sauce
¼ teaspoon salt
¼ teaspoon sugar
1 tablespoon vegetable oil
¾ cup vegetable or chicken broth
¼ cup pimiento strips, drained

•Cut woody stems from broccoli. Peel stems. Cut stems diagonally into slices. Cut broccoli tops into flowerettes; set aside. Cut onion into wedges. Cut celery diagonally into ¼-inch-thick slices. Rinse bean sprouts and drain. Finely chop garlic. Set aside.

•Combine cornstarch, water, oyster sauce, salt and sugar in small bowl; stir until smooth. Set aside.

•Heat wok over high heat about 1 minute or until hot. Drizzle oil into wok and heat 30 seconds. Add broccoli stems, onion and celery. Stir-fry 2 to 3 minutes or until vegetables are crisp-tender. Add broccoli flowerettes, garlic and broth. Cover wok and cook about 3 minutes or until broccoli is crisp-tender.

•Stir cornstarch mixture until smooth. Add to wok. Cook and stir until sauce boils and thickens.

•Add bean sprouts and pimiento to wok; stir-fry just until heated through. Transfer to serving dish.

Makes 6 servings

Stir-Fried Broccoli

STIR–FRIED TOFU AND VEGETABLES

½ pound firm tofu
1 medium yellow onion
1 cup vegetable oil
1 medium zucchini, cut into
    1-inch pieces
1 medium yellow squash, cut into
    1-inch pieces
½ cup sliced mushrooms
1 small red bell pepper, cut into
    ¼-inch strips

1 package (6 ounces) frozen snow
    peas, thawed
¼ cup water
2 tablespoons soy sauce
2 tablespoons tomato paste*
¼ teaspoon salt
⅛ teaspoon black pepper

•Drain tofu on paper towels. Cut crosswise into ¼-inch-thick slices. Set aside.

•Cut onion into 8 wedges; set aside.

•Heat oil in wok over medium-high heat about 5 minutes or until hot. Add tofu and fry about 8 minutes per side or until golden brown, turning once. Remove tofu with slotted spatula to baking sheet lined with paper towels; drain. Drain all but 2 tablespoons oil from wok.

•Add onion to wok and stir-fry 1 minute. Add zucchini, squash and mushrooms; stir-fry 6 to 7 minutes until zucchini and squash are crisp-tender, stirring occasionally.

•Add red pepper, snow peas and water to wok. Stir-fry 2 to 3 minutes or until crisp-tender. Stir in soy sauce, tomato paste, salt and black pepper until well mixed. Add tofu; stir-fry until heated through and coated with sauce. Transfer to serving dish.

Makes 4 servings

Remaining tomato paste may be transferred to small resealable plastic food storage bag and frozen.

❧❀☙

*T*ofu is high in protein, making it an ideal substitution for beef,
poultry or seafood.

Stir-Fried Tofu and Vegetables

SQUASH MEDLEY

2 small zucchini
2 small yellow squash
1 small red bell pepper, stemmed and seeded
1 piece fresh ginger (about ¾ inch square)

2 cloves garlic
½ cup vegetable or chicken broth
2 teaspoons cornstarch
¼ teaspoon salt
1 tablespoon vegetable oil
1 teaspoon butter or margarine

• Rinse zucchini and squash and pat dry with paper towels. Cut zucchini and squash diagonally into ¼-inch-thick slices. Cut pepper halves lengthwise into ¼-inch-thick strips. Finely chop ginger and garlic. Combine broth, cornstarch and salt in cup; stir until smooth.

• Heat wok over medium-high heat until hot. Drizzle oil into wok and add butter; swirl to coat bottom. Add ginger and stir-fry 30 seconds. Add zucchini and squash and stir-fry about 6 minutes or until crisp-tender. Stir in pepper and garlic; stir-fry 1 minute.

• Stir cornstarch mixture until smooth and add to vegetables. Stir-fry until sauce boils and thickens. Transfer to serving plate. *Makes 4 servings*

MONTEREY POTATO HASH

4 small baking potatoes
1 medium red onion
1 small green bell pepper
2 cloves garlic
2 tablespoons olive oil
1 teaspoon dried basil *or* oregano leaves, crushed

¼ teaspoon salt
¼ teaspoon black pepper
1 cup water
1 cup cherry tomatoes
¼ cup shredded Monterey Jack cheese

• Scrub potatoes and pat dry with paper towels. Cut potatoes crosswise into ¼-inch-thick slices. Slice red onion. Cut green pepper lengthwise in half. Remove stem and seeds; discard. Rinse, dry and cut into ¼-inch strips. Chop garlic.

• Heat wok over high heat about 1 minute or until hot. Drizzle oil into wok and heat 30 seconds. Add potatoes and stir-fry about 8 minutes or until lightly browned. Reduce heat to medium. Add onion, garlic, basil, salt and black pepper to potatoes; stir-fry 1 minute. Stir in water; cover wok and cook potatoes about 5 minutes or until tender, gently stirring once.

• Rinse tomatoes and pat dry with paper towels. Cut tomatoes in half; set aside. Add green pepper to potato mixture; stir-fry until all water evaporates in wok. Gently stir in tomatoes; heat through. Transfer to serving dish and sprinkle with cheese. *Makes 4 to 6 servings*

Squash Medley

ZESTY MIXED VEGETABLES

8 ounces green beans
½ small head cauliflower
2 green onions with tops
2 cloves garlic
1 or 2 jalapeño or Thai chili
    peppers*
2 tablespoons vegetable oil
8 ounces peeled fresh baby carrots

1 cup ⅓-less-salt chicken broth,
    divided
1 tablespoon cornstarch
2 tablespoons oyster sauce
1 teaspoon sugar
¼ teaspoon salt
    Red and yellow bell pepper strips
    for garnish

•Trim ends and remove any strings from beans; discard. Cut beans diagonally into thirds or quarters. Cut cauliflower into flowerettes. Cut onions into ½-inch pieces; keep white part and green tops of onions in separate piles. Chop garlic. Cut jalapeño lengthwise in half; remove stem and seeds. Cut jalapeño crosswise into thin slices.

•Heat wok over high heat about 1 minute or until hot. Drizzle oil into wok and heat 30 seconds. Add white part of onions, beans, cauliflowerettes, garlic and jalapeño; stir-fry until tender. Add carrots and ¾ cup broth. Cover wok and heat to a boil. Reduce heat to low and cook until carrots and beans are crisp-tender.

•Combine remaining ¼ cup broth, cornstarch, oyster sauce, sugar and salt in cup; stir until smooth. Stir into wok. Cook until sauce boils and thickens. Stir in onion tops. Transfer to serving dish. Garnish, if desired.   *Makes 4 servings*

Use 1 jalapeño for mild vegetables and 2 for hot vegetables.

❧❦❧

---

*J*alapeños are a small, dark green chili, normally 2 to 3 inches long and about ¾ inches wide with a blunt or slightly tapered end. Jalapeño flavor varies from hot to very hot. Use 1 to 2 in this dish depending on your preference.

---

*C*hilies can sting and irritate the skin; wear rubber gloves when handling chilies and do not touch eyes. Wash hands after handling chilies.

Zesty Mixed Vegetables

EGGPLANT ITALIANO

1¼ pounds eggplant
2 medium onions
2 ribs celery
½ cup pitted ripe olives
2 tablespoons olive oil, divided
1 can (16 ounces) diced tomatoes, drained
1 tablespoon sugar

1 tablespoon capers, drained
2 tablespoons balsamic vinegar
1 teaspoon dried oregano *or* basil leaves, crushed
Salt and black pepper
Fresh basil leaves, leaf lettuce and red jalapeño pepper for garnish

•Cut eggplant into 1-inch cubes. Thinly slice onions. Cut celery into 1-inch pieces. Cut olives crosswise in half.

•Heat wok over medium-high heat until hot. Drizzle 1 tablespoon oil into wok and heat 30 seconds. Add onions and celery and stir-fry about 2 minutes or until tender. Move onions and celery up side of wok. Reduce heat to medium.

•Add remaining 1 tablespoon oil and eggplant to wok. Stir-fry eggplant about 4 minutes or until tender. Add tomatoes and mix well. Cover wok and cook 10 minutes.

•Stir olives, sugar, capers, vinegar and oregano into eggplant mixture. Season with salt and pepper to taste. Transfer to serving dish. Garnish, if desired.   *Makes 6 servings*

*L*ook *for firm eggplants with smooth skin and a uniform color. They should be heavy for their size and flesh should bounce back when pressed with fingers. Usually, smaller eggplants are sweeter and more tender than larger ones.*

Eggplant Italiano

TOFU STIR–FRY

1 **pound firm tofu, drained**	1 **tablespoon soy sauce**
4 **tablespoons cornstarch, divided**	1 **tablespoon dry sherry**
8 **ounces broccoli**	1 **teaspoon sesame oil**
8 **ounces mushrooms**	½ **teaspoon salt**
1 **cup baby corn**	¼ **cup vegetable oil**
1 **can (14½ ounces) vegetable broth**	**Chow mein noodles**

•Dry tofu on paper towels. Cut tofu into 1-inch cubes. Place 2 tablespoons cornstarch on waxed paper. Coat tofu with cornstarch.

•Cut broccoli tops off woody stems; discard stems. Cut larger flowerettes into 2 × ½-inch pieces. Slice mushrooms. Cut corn in half.

•Combine broth, remaining 2 tablespoons cornstarch, soy sauce, sherry, sesame oil and salt in small bowl; stir until smooth.

•Heat wok over medium-high heat until hot. Drizzle vegetable oil into wok and heat 30 seconds. Ease tofu into hot oil and stir-fry about 10 minutes or until golden brown on all sides. Place tofu in large bowl. Reduce heat to medium.

•Add broccoli, mushrooms and corn to wok and stir-fry until mushrooms are tender. Cover wok and cook 3 minutes or until broccoli is crisp-tender. Stir cornstarch mixture until smooth and add to wok. Cook, uncovered, until sauce boils and thickens. Return tofu to wok; stir gently to mix. Transfer to serving dish. Serve over noodles.

Makes 4 servings

*T*ofu is puréed soybeans pressed to form a white custardlike cake. Tofu can be used in all kinds of recipes because it readily absorbs the flavor of other foods.

Tofu Stir-Fry

CARROTS CHINOISE

8 ounces medium carrots, peeled
2 teaspoons vegetable oil
¼ cup water
1 package (6 ounces) frozen Chinese
    pea pods, partially thawed

1 can (8 ounces) sliced water
    chestnuts, drained
1 teaspoon sesame oil
½ teaspoon salt
⅛ teaspoon black pepper

• Cut carrots diagonally into thin slices.

• Heat wok over medium-high heat until hot. Drizzle vegetable oil into wok and heat 30 seconds. Add carrots and stir-fry until lightly browned. Reduce heat to medium.

• Add water; cover wok and cook about 4 minutes or until carrots are crisp-tender.

• Add pea pods, water chestnuts, sesame oil, salt and pepper to wok. Stir-fry until pea pods are heated through. Transfer to serving dish.

Makes 4 servings

STIR–FRIED GREENS AND BEANS

8 ounces bok choy *or* Swiss chard
8 ounces napa cabbage
4 romaine lettuce leaves
1 large onion
2 cloves garlic
6 slices bacon
2 tablespoons olive oil or vegetable
    oil

1 teaspoon dried oregano leaves,
    crushed
½ teaspoon salt
⅛ teaspoon crushed red pepper
1 can (16 ounces) white kidney
    beans, drained and rinsed
Hot cooked ziti or penne
Grated Parmesan cheese

• Separate bok choy leaves from stems. Rinse and drain. Cut bok choy stems diagonally into ½-inch slices. Cut bok choy leaves crosswise into 1-inch slices. Keep leaves and stems in separate piles. Rinse cabbage and cut crosswise into ½-inch slices. Rinse romaine leaves and drain. Tear leaves into 2-inch pieces. Slice onion and chop garlic. Cut bacon slices crosswise into 1-inch pieces.

• Heat wok over medium-high heat until hot. Add bacon and stir-fry until crisp and brown. Remove bacon to small bowl and discard all but 1 tablespoon bacon fat. Drizzle oil into wok and heat 30 seconds. Add onion and bok choy stems and stir-fry 2 minutes.

• Add garlic, oregano, salt, red pepper and beans to wok; stir-fry until beans are heated. Add bok choy leaves, cabbage and romaine; stir-fry until greens are wilted. Transfer to serving bowl; sprinkle with bacon. Serve with pasta. Sprinkle with cheese.

Makes 4 to 6 servings

Carrots Chinoise